IT'S TIME
FOR A TALK

It's Time
for a Talk

Donald L. Engel

To order additional copies of this book, contact:
Xlibris Corporation
1-888-795-4274
www.Xlibris.com
Orders@Xlibris.com
136532

TABLE OF CONTENTS

PROLOGUE

I answered a knock at our door one afternoon, and it was two Jehovah's Witnesses. I explained that I was an Atheist, and wasn't interested in their literature. Although I was polite, they immediately spun around as if I had slapped them in the face, and scurried down the walk. When I closed the door, I sat down and wondered how they would feel if someone came to their home and tried to hand them literature on Atheism. It made me stop and think about how religion was trying to guide and govern our lives. Then I thought about all the problems concerning abortion, prayer in school, religious statues on government land, The Ten Commandments depicted on the Justice Building, homosexual rights, the Evangelists trying to wedge their way into politics, and all the rest of it that we've heard and read so much about lately. I think it is about time that we sit down and talk in a sane, sensible manner about some of these ideas. This is my attempt to start the conversation. This book describes my thoughts, and how I came to think this way.

the other hand, poor dietary habits and pubertal hormonal changes increase the adolescents' risk for tooth decay and gingival inflammation. Therefore, oral hygiene procedures are very important at this age, and the role of the parents to encourage their grudging adolescents to carry out their duties is extremely important.

ACKNOWLEDGEMENT

I want to thank a close friend, who wishes to remain anonymous, for his willingness to help me in writing this work by spending untold hours editing and keeping me on track, even though he does not subscribe to many of the ideas expressed herein.

Thanks, Art.

INTRODUCTION

When I was 17, my paternal grandmother passed away at the age of 63 from a stroke. She was the most devout Catholic I've ever known. She went to morning and evening Mass every day, walking about a half mile each way to get there, rain, shine, or snow. She always had a rosary in her hand, and was constantly saying her "Hail Marys". She had the crucifix on her walls in every room, along with candles, pictures of Jesus, and Mother Mary. Her husband was put in a mental institution when my dad was very young, so she had to raise 5 children on her own at a time when women didn't work. If I remember correctly, the last job she had was working in a potato chip plant, but I don't know what she did other than I know it wasn't an office job. She was a very hard worker, and once her children were raised she put her money into buying a boarding house. She continued working, and by combining her wages with the money she made from boarders, at the time of her death, she was able to give a house to each of her children.

My aunt would call her every morning just about the time she got home from Mass to make sure she was okay. One morning she called and there was no answer. She waited a while and called again, and still no answer, so she called the priest at the church. He hadn't seen her at mass that morning, and was wondering why. Then my aunt called grandma's neighbor and asked her to check on grandma. The neighbor found grandma passed out on the kitchen floor, called for an ambulance, and then called my aunt and told her what she found.

By seeing the evidence, it was determined that she had had a stroke the day before, and it looked like it happened just after my aunt had talked to her. That means that she had lain on the cold kitchen floor for over 24 hours with no way to communicate her plight. She died in the hospital two days later without ever regaining full consciousness.

Although I believed in God at the time, I didn't go to church. I had gone to Catholic school during the fall semester of the third grade, but then we moved and from then on it was only public schools. But it really bothered me that here was the most religious person I'd ever met, and not just because she went to church every day, but she lived the Christian life every minute of the waking day, and God had let her lay on that cold floor for 24 hours with no way to communicate. Of course I'm older now, and I realize that compared to what other people who are just as faithful have endured, laying on a cold floor for 24 hours is minor. But at the time, it struck me as a lousy way to treat someone that spent her entire life adoring her God!! Where is the love that is attributed to God? This didn't seem to make sense, and I begin to have doubts.

Then, a couple of years later, my cousin (the same grandmother's granddaughter) came down with breast cancer. It was in the early '60s, so there was no hope of a cure for her. She died a long, slow, painful death. She was also a devout Catholic, who attended mass at every chance she could. She was a working woman, so she couldn't make morning mass, but when time would allow, she went to evening mass. Here is another case where a life of adoration was repaid with over a year of pure pain. That's not a loving God. He's beginning to look like a sadistic God!! He seems to be cruelest to the ones that love Him the most.

For a couple of years after that, I would ask every priest or minister that I met why God was treating his adorers that way. Some would say, "We're being tested.", and my question is, "Tested for what?". Here are two women that spent their whole lives believing, loving, trusting, and adoring. Tested for what?

Then a few years later, my wife's grandmother died a long, slow death from cancer of the female organs. She was another of the most religious people I had ever met. My wife has a 40-year old niece who is another wonderful Christian. She doesn't talk about religion, she just leads a perfect Christian life and runs a Christian home with her husband and three children. She came down with breast cancer and had a double massive mastectomy. A year later, her 18 year old daughter was also diagnosed with breast cancer. Here are five women who could not have led more Christian-like lives than they did, and for their efforts were treated in the most abominable way. Tested for what? Was he mistreating those five women to test me for my reaction? Or was he testing them?

Why would they need to be tested? They had just given their whole lives to Him, so what else could be asked of them? To me, "testing" doesn't seem like a plausible answer.

Other priests and ministers were more honest about it, and would admit that they didn't know why things are the way they are. If they don't know, why are they telling me I should believe? If you can live in this world and see the madness and injustice, how can anyone possibly preach that God is loving and caring? Where is the evidence for these statements? Every indication I've seen is that life is a crap shoot, or God is a sadist. Either way, it doesn't jibe with what the religious leaders are saying.

The Bible says that God created man in his own image. Obviously, since He is a spirit, we can't look like Him physically, so it must mean that we have minds that work like His. We have the same sense of right and wrong, and the same sense of justice. And again, according to the Bible, He has talked to several men throughout the Old Testament, so our words must have the same meanings to Him as they do to us. If that is so, the word "sadist" must mean the same to God and man. Since we have the same sense of justice, why is He treating so many truly good people with such total injustice?

When you bring up the subject of this inconsistency between what is taught in church, and what is observed in life, the minister will tell you that you should ignore the pain that you see on earth, because we will receive our rewards in heaven. In the Old Testament, there is not one word that would indicate anyone is going to heaven for any reason. That was God's realm, and no human was going to get there by body, soul, or any other way. In fact, Adam and Eve were kicked out of the Garden of Eden just to make sure they could not eat from the tree of life, and become like the gods and have eternal life. No one alive has ever been to heaven or hell, so there is absolutely no indication or confirmation that either of those places actually exist. I agree with you that it seems a waste to gain all this knowledge and experience and have it all go to waste when we die. And I also agree with you that I hope something is there to continue when we die, but there is absolutely no indication that there is.

Probably the most famous Catholic in the modern world, Mother Teresa of Calcutta, started having the same doubts about the existence of God soon after starting her charity work. She was born in Albania, and after becoming a Catholic nun, devoted her life to helping the poor, sick, downtrodden, and orphans in Calcutta, India from 1950 until her death in 1997. For her work, she was awarded the Nobel Peace Prize in

1979. She was unable to match the lives of these people with God's love that is expressed by the church. Throughout this entire period until her death, she wrote letters to her superiors explaining her doubts about the existence of God. (Google "Mother Teresa's religious beliefs").

Think of all the people in the world who believe in one god or another. There are so many gods, but which is the correct one? They do want to believe, and they want to believe in the correct god. Why doesn't God talk to man any more? Since there are so many religions that have opposing ideas, why doesn't He come down and light the burning bush again and explain to us what He really wants? Just think of all the truly devout religious people dying in wars over religion. In New York on 9/11/2001, approximately 3000 people died in one battle of a religious war. He could stop all of it now with a little talk. What is your word for it?

Although there have been many instances of near death experiences described by people who almost died, there is no way to confirm that what they saw or experienced was reality. Of course, the religious say they peered into heaven, and saw family and friends waiting there to greet the person having the experience. Even atheists have had comparable visions. Many of the non-religious, and the religious say they came to a bright light. An interesting point about these near death experiences is that many Catholics have reported seeing the Virgin Mary, but not one Protestant or atheist has ever reported this phenomenon. It appears to me that during these near death experiences, you are going to see what you expect to see, or want to see. For instance, at least one person said he saw his deceased friends, family, and his DOGS!!! If you are going to accept these near death experiences as proof of heaven, then you have to accept the fact that dogs also have souls and go to heaven.

I read the Catholic Bible from front cover, word for word, to the back cover, and then the Protestant Bible from front cover, word for word, to the back cover. I could find nothing to convince me that my thinking was wrong, and so after all the studying, I became an Atheist. It's easier to not believe in Him at all, than to believe He is sadistic. I treat my friends, and even those who I do not like, better than He treats His adorers. I try to be a good person to everyone because it feels right, not because I'm afraid of what will happen to me if I'm not.

Atheists have good times and bad times. The religious have good times and bad times. There is not one shred of evidence that there is any rhyme or reason for any of it. No evidence of any master plan. No evidence of outside influence. Nothing.

When I sat back and thought about all that I had read in the Bible, I realized that God didn't make man in His image. Man made God in his image. He used this God to explain everything that they couldn't understand at the time. The earth was the center of the universe, because everything was going around it. The earth is rotating on its axis at about 1,000 miles an hour, but they had no way of knowing that. The sun rose in the east, and set in the west. The next morning the sun came up in the east again. It must have gone completely around the earth to come back up in the east again. Not only the sun, but the moon and all the stars, in other words, the firmament, went around the earth too. The earth is the center of the universe!!

Then, in 1543, Copernicus published a book explaining his theory that the earth not only spun on its own axis, but spun around the sun, and therefore the sun was the center of the universe.

In 1633, Galileo, with his newly-invented telescope, demonstrated that the earth actually did rotate around the sun, and was duly sentenced by the Inquisition to house arrest for the rest of his life for teaching this heresy. He wasn't pardoned by the Church until 360 years later in 1992.

With the improvement of the telescope, further, and more detailed observation proved Copernicus' theory about the sun being the center of the universe was wrong, and today the actual center of the universe is still not known, and may never be. Religious theory, like scientific theory, must give way when solid, hard evidence proves it wrong.

Once I became an Atheist, the whole world seemed easier to accept. The randomness of nature made more sense, and was easier to work with. I no longer needed the "crutch" of religion to help me understand why I lost a loved one, or to get through life with its ever-expanding knowledge that seemed to oppose the teachings of an antiquated Bible.

Or, maybe even more importantly, in realizing the willingness of the religious right to interpret the Bible so as to control the actions of mankind that are continually influenced by new knowledge and technologies, and realizing their willingness to determine what is moral or immoral for everyone else, whether or not there is a basis in the Bible for their determinations.

1

MORALS

When the subject comes up that I am an Atheist, quite often a Christian will ask me, "If you don't believe in God, how do you know right from wrong?", or, "How can you be moral?"

Obviously, since morals are brought up so often, I have to ask, "Morals?" Whose morals? Why are your morals more moral than mine? Just who is it that is doing the judging between your morals and mine? Who assigned the Church to be the sole determination of morality?

Webster's definition of "moral" is:

1. Relating to, dealing with, or capable of making the distinction between, right and wrong in conduct. 2. relating to, serving to teach, or in accordance with, the principles of right and wrong 3. good or right in conduct or character; sometimes, specif., virtuous sexual conduct.

*SYN.—*moral *implies conformity with the generally accepted standards of goodness or rightness in conduct or character, sometimes, specif, in sexual conduct (a moral woman)* ethical *implies conformity with an elaborated, ideal code of moral principles, sometimes, specif., with the code of a particular profession (an ethical lawyer);* virtuous *implies a morally excellent character, connoting justice, integrity, and often, specif., chastity;* righteous *implies a being morally blameless or justifiable (righteous anger).*

I've heard it stated that a moral act is that act which does the most good, or at worst, the least amount of harm. The first part of that sentence is easy to understand. Helping a child across a busy street would be better than just standing there and wondering if he/she is going to make it on their own. Helping the child does the most good, and is therefore, a moral act.

But what about an act that does the least amount of harm? Sometimes that isn't so easy to see, or understand. Picture yourself on a ship that has just hit a coral reef, and is sinking. It goes lower into the water until it is just barely floating, and seems to maintain that level of buoyancy. Everyone is clinging to the ship, when you hear knocking on the bulkhead behind a sealed hatch. You hear a couple of people screaming to be let out. There are 3,000 people clinging to the ship, and two or three inside wanting to get out, and you know they will drown if you don't let them out. Here is the dilemma—If you open the hatch to let them out, you might be releasing the pocket of air that is keeping the ship afloat, and therefore assigning the fate of 3002 people to death by drowning. Obviously, the moral act is to let the two inside the ship drown, rather than drowning everyone. It is the act which does the least amount of harm. Every sailor who has made it through basic training has been taught this lesson in morality.

Many native tribes in the Amazon jungle believe that a child born with a deformity has no soul, and that the child should be buried alive, poisoned, or left in the jungle to die. That is their moral code. We couldn't live with it, but that is what they feel is right for their society. And in some cases it might be a necessity for the survival of the tribe. If the deformity is so serious that the child would never be able to contribute to their society, it would have to be taken into consideration that the tribe probably doesn't produce enough to carry the burden of non-producing members. Since the act allows the tribe to survive, it meets the definition of an act that does the least amount of harm.

The Followers of Christ, a fundamentalist Christian denomination in Oregon, believe in faith healing. They let their children die from readily treatable diseases. Is that moral? Not in my mind!! And yet, they are a Christian denomination, so they must be moral. Right??

We're all aware of the problems the Catholic church is having with child molestation by several priests over the past several years. As I am writing this very paragraph, they just had on the news that the coach at Nazareth High School (a private Catholic school in New York) molested several of the boys in his classes. Is that moral? Not in my mind!! I want to say here that the problem is not only in the Catholic church, but all of them. Evangelist Tony Alamo was convicted of child molestation, Evangelist Ted Haggard hired a gay prostitute, Evangelist Jerry Falwell bought the services of a prostitute, or Evangelist Jim Bakker who was involved in a sex scandal, and then went to prison for accounting fraud. I only mentioned the Catholic church because it has been covered so much in all the news media, so everyone is aware of it.

But before I leave the Catholic church, let me tell you about another "moral" act committed by the Catholic priesthood. How many of you are aware of the priests castrating male choir boys who had contralto and soprano voices during the Middle Ages? According to one source, the practice continued until the early 20th century. The purpose was to provide the high notes that only girls can normally attain, but since girls weren't allowed to be in the Catholic choir, they had to use castrated boys to provide these high notes.

You and I know it is immoral, and I don't have to believe in God to know it.

Looking at the synonyms of moral; *moral* implies conformity with the _generally accepted standards of goodness or rightness in conduct or character._ (Emphasis mine). In other words, society as a whole, sets the moral code, not some religious denomination. Do you want to follow the moral code of The Followers of Christ, and pray over your sick child instead of taking the child to the doctor?

And so, I ask again. Morals? Whose morals? Who is the judge that will decide whose morals are correct? Society, as a whole, decides what is or is not moral. While some groups, or individuals, feel their morals are higher than others, that is only for them to decide for themselves, and may not be agreed to by the rest of the population.

The Followers of Christ, who let their children die of treatable diseases, think they are moral. The rest of us think they're immoral nuts. On July 31, 2009, Carl Brent Worthington of Oregon City, Oregon, and a member of that church, was sentenced to 2 months in jail plus 5 years of probation, for allowing his 15 month old daughter to die from a cyst on her throat without seeking medical attention. Society did not accept his idea of morality, and sentenced him. Society set the moral code, not religion.

On Dec 10, 2009, it was reported that a couple in the Portland, OR area received 7 years in prison for child abuse. They said they weren't abusing their children, they were disciplining them according to scripture. Society set the moral code, not religion.

It's one thing for an adult to refuse medical help, and ask his family and friends to gather around him and try to cure him of an illness with prayers. It is quite another to force a child to go through a painful dying process when the child has no understanding of life, death, good, bad, or any of the other things that are taken into consideration when making life and death decisions.

On February 3, 2010, Jeff and Marci Beagley, another couple from the same church were found guilty of not seeking medical help in the death of their 16-year-old son. He died of a urinary tract blockage. Society set the moral code, not religion. If you are a male, and wonder what kind of pain was forced on that kid, it would be like tying a string around your penis and leaving it there until you died. That is a "Christian family" that forced that pain and death on a son they supposedly loved.

Man is a social animal by nature. In early times, man had to stick together or become food for other animals. Most larger animals can run faster than man. Most animals have a better sense of smell than man. Most animals of any size are stronger than man, And so man had to stick together in packs for survival. From that time on, we've built up a set of social rules that allow us to live together in close proximity with some sense of harmony. We call these rules "morals".

Morality is knowing the difference between what society has deemed right and wrong. Since society makes the determination of what is right and wrong, it's not necessary to be religious to be moral. And society's morals change with time, knowledge, and understanding. Look at the spreading acceptance of homosexual marriage. If Christianity can't advance and adapt with increasing knowledge, it will continue to lose its significance in society, and the percentage who are Christian, which is currently about 75 percent, will continue to drop.

While society sets the moral code for society as a whole, we've often heard someone say they can't go along with something because it is against their own personal moral code. There are acts that might be accepted by society as a whole, but not accepted by an individual. Abortion is the most obvious example of such an act.

2

ABORTION

Abortion has been around, and in continuous practice, since at least the time of Classical Greece. Hippocrates died 370 years BC, Plato, who died about 348 years before Christ was born, and Aristotle, who died 322 years BC, all mentioned the subject. The Roman, Pliny the Elder, lived during Jesus' time and mentioned several recipes for the specific purpose of causing abortion, and yet there is no mention of abortion anywhere in the Old or New Testament.

Pro-lifers feel that at the moment of conception, the first multiplying cells are human, and it immediately has a soul. I don't know where they got this idea. The Bible (Genesis 2:7) says God breathed the breath of life into Adam <u>after</u> he had formed him. The Catholic Bible, and the Jewish Torah say, "*and he became a living being*", while The Protestant King James version says, "and he became a living soul". No matter which word you want to use, "being" or "soul", Adam did not become a being or soul until after he was formed.

Again, in Job. Job was a well-to-do man with a large family, and home. He had many animals and many servants. But one day God allowed Satan to do what he wanted with Job to prove that Job was faithful. Satan caused Job to lose his animals, servants, children, and finally his home. Obviously, Job was completely destroyed. From Job 3:1 to 3:9 he laments, and curses the day he was born. He asked why wasn't he stillborn so that he never would have had to live.

Then in Job 3:16, he states: "*Or as an hidden untimely birth <u>I had not been</u>; as infants which never saw light.*" (Emphasis mine.)

Exodus 21:22-25 seems to corroborate this thought.

"22 If men quarrel, and one strike a woman with child, and she miscarry indeed, but live herself: he shall be answerable for so much damage as the woman's husband shall require, and as arbiters shall award. 23 But if her death ensue thereupon, he shall render life for life. 24 Eye for eye, tooth for tooth, hand for hand, foot for foot, 25 Burning for burning, wound for wound, stripe for stripe."

Because it doesn't have a soul yet, God places no importance on the fetus, and leaves it to the father for resolution. This passage indicates "Thou shalt not kill" has no bearing concerning the fetus, because the fetus hasn't received its soul yet. This is evident in the way the death of the mother would be handled, if she died, in comparison to the death of the fetus.

Aristotle stated that the fetus received its soul 40 days after conception if it was male, and 90 days if it was female. St. Augustine, 354-430 CE, agreed with that theory, and St. Thomas Aquinas, 1225-1274 CE, also accepted that idea.

I remember an incident when I was 7 years old. I was at a friend's house, and one of the adults in the house was talking about a friend having a baby, and made the statement, "The baby took in its soul at 4:30 this morning." Now that was an interesting statement!! What is a soul? And why did the baby take it in? I went home, and asked my mother what that was all about, and she said that means the baby took its first breath and became a person at 4:30. This happened about the time that President Franklin Roosevelt died, so it wasn't that long ago that people had a completely different idea of when a fetus became a baby.

I feel that a person's soul is his/her entire thought process, including thoughts, memory, mental stature, and mental reactions to any stimuli. A person's very essence, or nature. In other words, the person has to have a brain to have thoughts, and the brain has to be developed enough to think to have a soul. A fetus does not have any kind of brain at all in the first trimester, let alone enough brain to have thoughts. It doesn't even have enough brain to feel pain until somewhere between the 28th and 30th week of gestation, and that's half way through the 3rd trimester!!

Since the moment of ensoulment is not stated anywhere in the Bible other than Genesis 2:7, and implied in Job 3:16, and Exodus 21:22, I choose to think that a fetus does not have a soul until it is born, breaths on its own, and starts to absorb and act on information. This thought seems to be in line with the Bible's description, and the feelings of the early church. It wasn't until the mid 1800's that the Catholic church decided that the fetus has a soul at the moment of conception.

In the early years of the Catholic church, abortion was evil only if it was used to hide "fornication or adultery". Later on it was considered murder if it was done after the fetus was "ensouled" that is to say, when it received its soul. (During this period, it was thought to be a different length of time after conception for males and females, before they were ensouled.) And it wasn't until about 160 years ago that the Church considered abortion as murder at any stage after conception. And even now, the Church has not made that an infallible decision. In other words, that is how they feel about it now, but they are allowing room for change in the future.

In the U.S., abortion was legal before "quickening", (That is before the mother felt the first movements by the fetus.), up until the 1820's. Connecticut passed the first law against apothecaries selling solutions for the sole purpose of causing abortions in 1821. In 1829, New York passed the first laws against abortions by making abortion a felony if committed after quickening, and a misdemeanor if done before.

No matter which side of the debate you are on, we've all heard the many different circumstances that might warrant an abortion; to save the mother's life, incest, to prevent the birth of a fetus with a known deformity, (such as Down's Syndrome that can be detected before birth), convenience, finances, curtails the mother's future, etc., etc., etc. Looking at these different circumstances, it must be realized that sometimes an abortion is the act that does the least amount of harm, and can be considered a moral act.

Part of the problem is that the Pro-Lifers appeal to emotion. They show a sonogram of a fetus in the womb that is close to birth and say, "It's a baby. See!! It has arms, and legs, and eyes, and a nose, and it's sucking on its thumb!!" Why don't they show a sonogram of a fetus in the first trimester, since that is when most abortions are performed?

Another part of the problem is that quite often when we think of abortion, we are visualizing teenagers getting abortions to correct mistakes made in the back seat. At the time we are thinking of this, we are not thinking of the mother of a Christian family with other children, who's pregnancy has developed into a life-threatening situation. I've heard it said that even when the mother's life is in danger, an abortion is not warranted. What kind of person could possibly ask their mother, sister, daughter, or wife, to give up their life for the sake of an unborn fetus? Only a person that cannot possibly get pregnant could demand such a sacrifice. That thought is so repugnant to me that I get angry every time I hear someone say it. If there is an epitome of fanaticism, this would have to be it. Where is the morality in depriving her other children of a mother? Which takes us back to morals. Whose morals? How can the death of the mother be considered the least amount of harm?

The Pro-lifer wants life, life, and more life without regard to the quality of the life the baby faces, or the future life of the mother, or the effect it will have on children already in the family, or the family as a whole. In many cases the mother already has other children, and she has to think of the quality of life for those children also. Where is the morality of forcing married (or any other) women, to have more children if they don't have the resources to properly take care of the children they already have? Where is the morality in forcing the mother of a family to accept death, when the fetus is going to die before birth, or shortly after birth?

The Pro-Lifers like to twist words and their meanings. On several occasions I've heard or read that using the stem cells from fetuses will result in "farming fetuses" for the sole purpose of obtaining stem cells. As if the fetuses were developed, and then aborted, for the sole purpose of getting their stem cells. Getting the stem cells is an indirect result of abortion, not the goal. And there are so many abortions, that it will never be necessary to "farm" fetuses for this purpose.

In another instance of twisting word meanings, I heard a Pro-Lifer state that abortion could be considered as a form of genocide, because minorities are the largest number of women getting abortions. (Percentage-wise by race.) (http://www.census.gov/compendia/statab/cats/births_deaths_marriages_divorces/family_planning_abortions.html)

Webster defines genocide as:

"The systematic killing or extermination of a whole people or nation."

Abortions are not systematic, and they are not aimed at any specific people or nation. The pregnant woman approaches the doctor. To be systematic, the doctor would have to approach the pregnant woman. Or there would have to be laws that only allow women of certain races to have abortions. None of that is taking place. Those who receive abortions approach the doctor of their own volition, and with their own, or their families' well being in mind. I seriously doubt if the pregnant mother, or the abortionist, is thinking of her race at the time of decision.

That is something statisticians do after the fact.

The following are reasons I think abortion can be moral, and should remain legal:

1. Whether it is legal, or illegal, if a woman wants an abortion, she will get it. Either in a dark alley with a "doctor", or a coat hanger. Before abortion was legalized, many young women bled to death when using an object, such as a coat hanger to try and scrape the fetus from their womb. Or died because of infection obtained in a less than sterile "operating" room.

2. Any woman that can afford to cross into Canada, or travel to Europe can get an abortion on demand. If I remember right, that was one of the arguments given when they legalized abortion with "Roe v. Wade". When abortions were illegal, they were only illegal for the poor women. The better off were flying to Europe, so it was seen as a "class" issue.

3. If the woman has an abortion, it means she doesn't want the baby. If she were forced to carry through with the baby, she would be raising a child she does not want. The chances of there being a bonding between her and the child are questionable. Think of everything you've heard of serial killers; it seems to me that almost everyone of them, if not all, said there was no bonding with their mother when they were children. I am not saying that every unwanted child born will turn into a serial killer, but it seems to me that if women are forced to carry through with an unwanted pregnancy to term, it will increase the number of dangerous misfits in our society.

Roe v. Wade was decided early in 1973. About 18 years later, the crime rate in all categories started a decline that continues to this day. (wikipedia.org/wiki/Legalized_abortion_and_crime_effect) There are several studies, both for and against this correlation, but the fact remains as stated.

4. I continually hear that adoption would be an alternative to abortion. In 2002, there were 52,534 adoptions. That same year 134,836 children under the age of 16 were still in foster homes after the adoptions.

If you are one of those who proposes adoption, I hope you are at the agency trying to adopt at least one of the remaining 134,836 children who haven't been adopted yet. If you're not, how can you possibly use that as a solution? (I heard President Bush say that adoption was an alternative, but I never heard any reports of him setting any examples of leadership by adopting a child.). The Pro-Lifers seem to be living in a dream world where everything is being taken care of by someone else. Believe me, IT'S NOT!! (A side note: There were 867,475 abortions in the year 2000. If they had been born, how many more children would still be in foster homes?)

5. The monetary drain on society to maintain children in foster homes is enormous. There are many reasons why children end up in foster homes, but why add to the load by forcing women to have babies they don't want?

6. The religious fanatics on the right don't want to give in any quarter. They say the wife must submit to the husband upon his demand. The wife cannot take a birth control pill, or use a condom, and then after sex she can't use the "morning after" pill, and if she gets pregnant, they don't want her to have an abortion. In other words, she is looked at as nothing more than a sex machine and baby factory.

7. Incest. It is against the law for a woman to marry her brother, father, (or first cousin in most states), because the chances for physical, or mental disability increases greatly in sex between close relatives. If we won't allow marriages for this reason, why should we force a woman to carry a pregnancy from incest through when the chances are so great for these disabilities? Does that make any sense?

Those of you who are pro life must think by now that I am cold-hearted, and uncaring about life. Actually, just the opposite is true. I just want to focus my attention on those who are already alive, and those WANTED pregnancies. It is hard for me to direct my thoughts and efforts toward an unwanted fetus, when we have to make a choice as to whether that unwanted fetus receives our resources, or the already born, and wanted, who are in need of help.

The head of Health and Human Services for Oregon stated that the state was strapped for people willing to provide foster care. As a result of this, they have been returning children to their birth parents in what can only be described as "doubtful circumstances". The statement was the end of an article on the death of a child who had been returned to his parents, even though the father was a convicted child molester, and the mother was a "meth" addict.

In 2004, a man from Silverton, Oregon was arrested for child abuse. He had gone to Romania and adopted a little boy. When the boy reached nine years old, the man took videos of himself performing sex acts on his adopted son. He returned the rented video camera before erasing the pictures. The next camera renter took the video to the police.

In two other cases where girls were adopted, one was 9 years old and weighed 26 1/2 pounds, and the other was adopted by another family. She was 5 years old and weighed 28 pounds.

The last four cases took place in a period of two weeks, and all of them happened in Oregon. Think about what is happening across the entire country!! Foster parents, and adoption do not always work.

We continuously hear people say, "If they would relax the adoptions rules, more kids would be adopted." The news stories I just told you about illustrate why there are such strict rules for adoption. I wonder if the man had tried to adopt in America, and was turned down, before going to Romania.

The cry of the Pro-lifer is, "Life is precious!". Yes, I agree life CAN be precious, but there are circumstances where allowing the life of a fetus to continue is the greater harm, as the preceding cases show.

God said, "Be fruitful, and multiply." Okay, we did that. Now what? We've multiplied to the point that we are so crowded that we are destroying the earth. Where is a practical solution? The Pro-lifers always have solutions, but I haven't heard a practical one yet. One other solution I heard President Bush state was 'abstinence'. Remember, that as some claim, the wife has to submit to her husband. Who is it that is supposed to abstain? Be honest—who wants to abstain?

There is such an ongoing interest concerning the morality of abortion, CNN had an article that covered two families, and how they handled the abortion issue. The first story was about a woman who was pregnant with twins, and the twins had "Twin to twin transfusion Syndrome". This meant that the twins were sharing all bodily fluids and it would be fatal to them. It could also be fatal to the mother if the pregnancy continued. The doctor, with the mother and husband, decided that an abortion was necessary to protect the mother. The abortion was carried out. In the second story, a mother was pregnant with a fetus that had problems with "Chromosome 18", it only had half a brain, and several other serious physical defects. She decided to carry the pregnancy to term. The baby lived for 12 hours. In both cases, the parents were comfortable with their decision, and the outcomes. And . . . more noteworthy . . . both women had been trying to get pregnant, so they did want their children. Neither couple wanted to terminate their pregnancy.

I just don't understand how a person of faith can have the audacity to tell a woman, who may be just as faithful, that she doesn't have the right to save her own life. Isn't that playing God? Aren't you trying to force a decision on someone according to your beliefs? Remember, they are only your beliefs, because there is nothing in the Bible about abortion. Why are your beliefs more valid than hers? Who gave you the right to make life and death decisions for other people? And if you do have that right, why doesn't the mother, who's life is in danger, have the same right?

The subject of abortion in the U.S. is a good example of the continuing development of morals within a society. We've gone, in a period of 150 years, from no restrictions on abortion until 1820, and then no abortions, (except to save the mother's life) until 1973, to no restrictions on abortion. Since the "Roe v. Wade" decision, society has been split almost exactly down the middle in its support/non-support of this decision. One survey will say it's 51% in favor, and then the next survey says 51% against, and it's been that way since the decision was made in 1973.

Since we can't seem to make up our minds, I obviously believe we should continue with "Freedom of choice". It doesn't force anyone to do something they don't want, and it allows those who feel it is morally okay to have the abortion, to do so without becoming a criminal.

And, trying to eliminate Freedom of Choice, by overturning Roe v. Wade is disgusting. What is the point? As I stated earlier, any woman who can afford to go into Canada, or to Europe can get an abortion on demand. I was amazed that all of the Republican candidates for president in the 2008 and 2012 presidential races, were proclaiming their intention to amend the Constitution in an effort to nullify "Roe v. Wade". Have they no sense of what America is about? Have they no sense of how America works? What are they doing running for president with so little understanding of American democracy, and the intention of the Constitution? (At the time of the writing of the U.S. Constitution, abortion was legal in all 13 states.)

The influence of the religious right on politics in the U.S. cannot be overestimated. Some states have already passed laws, (contestable), limiting or prohibiting abortion. Others are considering it. This flies in the face of the U.S. Supreme Court decision to permit unrestricted abortions in "Roe v. Wade."

The Republican party has been torn asunder because of their desire to get the Evangelist's vote. The Evangelists won't give their vote unless the politician agrees that "Roe v. Wade" must be overturned. And the rest of the nation won't vote for anyone who is going to try and overturn that decision.

The religious right is complaining that the Supreme Court is way too liberal. It isn't—they're arriving at their judgments the way the law was meant to be. Just because it doesn't follow what the Evangelists want, it doesn't mean it is wrong. The Constitution tries to allow as much freedom as possible. It is the Evangelists who want to be so repressive, and restrictive.

Former Governor Palin of Alaska not long ago announced that she is going to try to start a movement that is to the right of center. Don't we have a Republican party that is already to the right of center? And didn't that party get trounced in the 2008 and 2012 elections?

I have been a Republican all of my 76-year old adult life, but the party has swung so far, socially, to the right, that I blindly voted straight down the Democratic ticket without even looking at the names. I found out later that I know two other people who did the same thing. If there are three of us (that I know of) in my circle of friends, how many across the nation did the same thing? It might explain why President Obama is having such a hard time getting the things passed that he had campaigned on. He thought that since he was elected on what he had been promising, that it was what the people wanted. He doesn't realize he was elected because of Republican protest votes.

The problem in the Republican party today is that all the candidates are trying to be good Christians, and what we need are good Americans. When I think of American leaders and their religion, I immediately think of John F. Kennedy. There were all kinds of scare tactics put out by the Republicans that implied that because Kennedy was Catholic, it meant the Pope would be running America through Kennedy. President Kennedy came out and made a public statement promising the citizens that if elected president, his religion would not interfere with his presidential duties or decisions.

Not only do today's Republican candidates not make a similar statement, they actually push their religion out in front, and state openly that they will do everything they can to influence the presidential office with their religion. We've been celebrating the separation of church and state for over 200 years, and now the Republicans and Evangelists want to bring them together.

In 2009, Representative Patrick Kennedy was refused communion by his priest because of his stance on pro-choice in the health care bill. To Representative Kennedy I say, "Hip Hip Hooray!!" It's nice to see he's following his uncle's example. It would be nice if we could find a Republican with such courage.

American society has always been divided almost equally on the abortion issue, so the courts have acted in the appropriate way. The Constitution was written to provide as much freedom as possible, and the courts have followed that idea by making the decision that allowed the freedom of choice.

3

THE RELIGIONS OF
OUR NATION'S FOUNDERS

How many times have you heard someone say, "Oh, why can't we get our nation back to its Christian beginnings?" Either they don't know what life was like under the Puritan rule, or they are of the same mindset as the Puritans. I feel most Evangelists are in this category.

While we were all in elementary school, we learned about the Pilgrims when we put on a play about them at Thanksgiving. But how many of you, as adults, went back to this subject to learn what it was all about? Do you remember learning about the Salem Witch Trials? That infamous series of events occurred under the Puritan rule, and gives you some idea of religion gone berserk. From June 10, 1692 until September 22, 1692, 19 people were hanged for witchcraft. On September 19, 1692 one man was pressed to death because he wouldn't plead guilty or not guilty to witchcraft. Several died in prison while they were finishing their sentences for witchcraft.

An earlier hanging incident involved "The Boston martyrs". They were four Quakers who were hung by the Puritans for practicing their religion in the Massachusetts Bay Colony around 1660. This event preceded the witch trials by 30 years. Many other Quakers were sentenced to death, but were allowed to leave the colony, and were whipped as they passed through each town on the way out.

No one over the age of 21 today will ever forget the horrors of 9/11. If you watch the news at all, you've seen the actions of the Taliban of Afghanistan and Pakistan. It's the same thing. Religious fanaticism. And now, the religious right would like to get back to that system.

It's important to know that when the Puritans came to America, they were literally running for their lives because of their religious views. Many of them had gone to Holland first, but even there it was a worrisome ordeal, and when the chance came to go to the "New Land", they jumped at the opportunity. And, when they arrived, they were troublesome to everyone else around them in the new land. I feel most of today's Evangelists are in this category.

The Puritans, (adherents of Calvinism), were so strict, they kicked Roger Williams, a Pilgrim and Baptist preacher, out of their Massachusetts colony, because his thoughts on religious freedom went against their grain. In fact, they were down on all Baptists, Catholics, Quakers, and most other organized religions. If you practiced any other religion than theirs, (Christian, or not), you could be sent to jail, fined, have your property taken from you, have your children taken from you, or hanged!!

For a more detailed description of what life was like in Virginia under the Puritans, google "Notes on the State of Virginia" by Thomas Jefferson. Query 17 in that work describes the religious atmosphere in and around Virginia before the U.S. Constitution was adopted. And, it wasn't just Virginia. Every colony had their own established religion. The last state to disestablish was Massachusetts in 1833. In other words, it was tried once and it didn't work. Actually, it was tried 13 times, and it didn't work! Why would anyone want to go back to something that was tried 13 times, and didn't work? A popular description of insanity is continuous repetition of a failed sequence of events expecting a different outcome each time.

One interesting side note here, the Puritans outlawed the celebration of Christmas. If a child missed school on Christmas day, he/she was expelled. I brought this up because today we hear from the Evangelists that the stores are taking Christ out of Christmas. Under the Puritans, there was no Christmas celebration of any kind.

After Williams was kicked out of Massachusetts, he, along with a few followers, then went on to establish the settlement of Providence. He was the first to establish a separation between church and government, and to establish religious freedom. But, by 1691, Providence also fell under the strict Calvinism of the Puritans.

The Founding Fathers of our nation had experienced this religious fervor, and made it a point to make sure there was no established religion at the federal level. During the Constitutional convention Madison's notes on August 30, 1787 stated:

"Mr. PINKNEY moved to add to the article:—"but no religious test shall ever be required as a qualification to any office or public trust under the authority of the U. States"

Mr. SHERMAN thought it unnecessary, the prevailing liberality being a sufficient security against such tests.

Mr. Govr. MORRIS & Genl. PINKNEY approved the motion. The motion was agreed to nem: con: and then the whole Article; N. C. only no-& Md. Divided."

They made it a strong point that the United States was NOT founded on the Christian religion. In fact, there is a document that states it in those exact words. Ten years later, in 1797, the United States entered into a treaty with Tripoli, in which Article 11 states:

> "As the government of the United States is not, in any sense, founded on the Christian religion; as it has in itself no character of enmity against the laws, religion or tranquility {sic} of Musselmen . . . it is declared . . . that no pretext arising from religious opinion shall ever produce an interruption of the harmony existing between the two countries."

This treaty was written by Joel Barlow, under Washington's presidency, and was ratified by Congress under John Adams, and signed by Adams. It was only the third time in our history that the Senate ratified a bill unanimously, and with no dissenting comments. I don't know how it can get any more plain than that!!

We are a nation made up mostly of Christians, and so in that sense you can say we are a Christian nation. But we are not a nation built on the Christian religion, or even Christian principles. We are a nation built on democratic principals, and the Puritans demonstrated that that isn't the Christian way.

The 18th century was considered the "Age of Enlightenment", when science was blossoming, and Deism and Unitarianism were the big ideas in religion. Many of our more famous Founding Fathers were Deists or Unitarians, (or both). If you google "Religion of our Founding Fathers", the following partial list can easily be found in several sources:

Deists: George Washington, Thomas Jefferson, James Madison, Benjamin Franklin, Ethan Allen, Thomas Paine.

Unitarians: Thomas Jefferson, Paul Revere, Thomas Paine*,
Benjamin Franklin*, Ethan Allen*, John Adams, John
Quincy Adams.*

**Those marked with an asterisk believed in both. All of them in
both lists were brought up in Christian households, and changed
their beliefs after maturing.*

Generally speaking, Deism believes in one God who created the universe, and everything in it and then walked away. There is no way of knowing what His thoughts are, or what He expects of man, if anything. They believe that Jesus was a great man, but was not divine, therefore they do not believe in the Trinity. They do not believe in miracles or the idea that the Bible is error free. In other words, they believe there is a God that created the universe, but not in the Christian or any other organized religious sense.

Again, generally speaking, Unitarians do not believe that Jesus is the son of God. They believe that Jesus was a great man but not a part of God, and they do not believe the Bible is without error. They do, however, encourage the study of science, philosophy, and other religions to get a better understanding of the world, and to help understand the meaning of life. Today, they accept the theory of evolution. Since Darwin hadn't been born yet, there was no publicized concept of evolution. Had there been, I'm sure most of the Deist and Unitarian Founding Fathers would have accepted Darwin's ideas. There are many Unitarians who are Atheists, or Deists, and this might explain why some of them show up on both lists.

Episcopal minister Bird Wilson of Albany, New York, gave a sermon in 1831 in Albany, NY. In that sermon, he complained that none of the presidents from Washington to Jackson had professed any Christian religion more than Unitarianism. He wrote that although President Washington would escort Martha to church, he would leave after the sermon when she went forward to receive communion. He, himself (Washington), never received communion. He was considered a Deist, at best. Although Wilson mentioned Jackson in this sermon, Jackson is listed as a Presbyterian in another source. Jackson fought in 13 duels before he became president, and killed a man in one of them. That certainly wouldn't meet today's Christian standards. I said that, and then I thought of all the doctors who provide abortions, being shot by Christians, so I guess things haven't changed that much.

Jackson's successor, Martin van Buren officially belonged to the Dutch Reformed Church, but Franklin Steiner, wrote a book *The Religious Beliefs of Our Presidents*, and in that work he listed Van Buren among "Presidents Whose Religious Views Are Doubtful." That means the United States did not have a Christian president until 1837, and even then it is questionable if we had one before 1841.

A side note here: Among the people considered to be "Founding Fathers" are John Jay and Patrick Henry, both of whom were very Christian men, and stated so openly. Neither was ever President of the U.S.

What I've tried to point out in this chapter is that the religious today seem to have some rosy, glorified picture of how great religion was for our Founding Fathers' time period. If they mean the Pilgrims and Puritans, I can tell you that it was so strict, that the backlash resulted in the Founding Fathers of our Nation-—those who formed the Declaration of Independence, and the Constitution of the United States, insisting that no religion would be established at the federal level. The key figures during that time period were not anywhere close to what Christians are today. I mentioned the sermon by Bird Wilson. For a general idea of what the rest of the people in government were like at that time, read the rest of his sermon by googling "Bird Wilson".

I find it amusing that Christians want to get back to the Christianity our nation was founded on, only to find out it wasn't. The reason they have this picture in their minds is that when they were doing their grade school play about that period, they were children and had no idea of what the play was about. In their minds, they pictured sitting down with the local Indians (the memorable part because that would be really exciting to sit with the Indians!) and sharing turkey and corn on the cob. Nothing was brought up about the religious hardships exerted by the puritans. There was no need to, because the children wouldn't have understood it anyway.

4

HOMOSEXUALITY

I explained earlier that I thought God was invented to explain things that they had no way of understanding at the time. Homosexuality was one of those things that could not be explained. But, in this case, instead of trying to explain it, they just said homosexuals have to die!! And Muslims still believe in this directive today, and act on it without hesitation.

When I was going to military tech school, one of my classmates (I'll call him Hank) was obviously gay. Then after graduating, we were both assigned to the same unit. It wasn't too many months after we arrived that I heard high heels clicking in the barracks hallway. (Women in the male barracks were forbidden at the time.) I looked out, and there was Hank in a knee-high dress, high heels, and his hair combed down in bangs. And wearing women's make up!!

I asked him what he was doing, and he answered that he was being kicked out of the Air Force for being "queer". And, since everyone was going to know about it by the end of the day, there was no purpose in playing the game any longer. It seems his boyfriend downtown turned him in to the commander for being gay, because Hank wouldn't move in with him. We sat down and talked about homosexuality for a couple of hours.

He explained that gays don't know why they are the way they are. And that the idea that they have a choice of sexual preference is completely false. It would be just as repulsive to him to have sex with a female, as it would be for me to have sex with another male. I asked him if he would change if he could, and he answered no. He was just as happy with men as I was with women, and since his brain is wired that way, he had no attraction to women. He was happy as he was.

We can't blame our ancestors for not being able to explain homosexuality. We still can't today. (The incident with Hank took place in 1961.) Although there are several different studies that might show the cause, there is nothing definite yet. The most promising clue seems to be that the hypothalamus gland is different in homosexuals, and this difference develops before birth. For a more in-depth explanation, go to the following URL:

http://allpsych.com/journal/homosexuality.html

I traveled all over the world during my military career, and no matter what country I was in, I saw gays. In Thailand, the gay men, (google "kathoeys") have a beauty pageant every year, and the winner's picture is published on the front page of the newspapers. Homosexuality is not frowned upon in Thailand.

In 1994 the American Psychological Association stated that, "homosexuality is neither a mental illness, nor a moral depravity. It is the way a portion of the population expresses human love and sexuality."

Since homosexuals are found in all nations and cultures around the world, you can say that homosexuality is a normal thing. The exact percentage of the population that is gay is unknown because, depending on their home country, they face ostracism or death if they are found out, so many of them "stay in the closet". But the percentage is small enough that to be homosexual is considered abnormal. Percentage guesstimates range from 2 to 20 percent. Dr. Kinsey said 10 percent of the male population is homosexual.

On September 24, 2007, Mahmud Ahmadinejad, the Iranian president, while addressing students and faculty at Columbia University said, "We do not have homosexuals in Iran like you do in your country." He was almost laughed off the podium. Since they still kill homosexuals as a government policy in most of the Middle East nations, it might explain why they don't have any. Or, maybe when a Muslim realizes he/she's gay, they move to a western nation to escape decapitation, or stoning.

Homosexuals aren't a threat to our society, we're just learning that their brains are wired differently, and now we're beginning to understand that they aren't a threat to us or our way of life. You either are, or you're not gay. It's not a choice, it's stamped on you before you are born. As with everything else the Evangelists don't understand, they feel they're being threatened or pushed by the gays. "If we allow gay marriage it will ruin the social fabric of our society!!".

On November 11, 2009, the Australian Capital Territory (Australia's equivalent of the District of Columbia) approved gay civil unions.

On November 14, 2009, a judge in Buenos Aires approved gay marriages. The mayor said he would not appeal the decision, and on November 16, two men were granted a marriage license.

On December 5, 2009, The Episcopal Church elected a lesbian priest to the position of Bishop in L. A.

On December 14, 2009 Houston elected a lesbian mayor.

On January 1, 2010 Massachusetts became the fifth state to legalize same sex marriage.

In 2013 Washington state approved same sex marriage.

They're being accepted, and the world is not falling apart. I guess the Evangelists were wrong. Again.

This is another instance where society is changing the moral standards, based on new knowledge and understanding. As we learn more about the subject, we realize that it is just one more instance where the Bible did what it could with the understanding they had at the time it was written. The problem is that the Evangelists are not able, or should I say willing, to accept the new information.

In March of 2013, the U.S. Supreme Court listened to arguments in two cases concerning homosexual marriage. The congresses of Uruguay and France debated the legalization of homosexual marriage, and in the first week of April, 2013, became the 13th, and 14th countries to adopt homosexual marriage worldwide. This is an obvious example of morals changing on a world-wide basis, and it is not the Church that is leading the change. In fact, it is the Church that is fighting this change all the way to the courts. Society sets the moral code, not the Church.

5

I DON'T WANT TO HEAR IT!!

When I was still working, (after retiring from the military), the business where I worked was a 24/7 operation, and one day our section got a new supervisor. She advised me that she was claiming seniority and taking Sundays off so she could attend church. I advised her that since I am an Atheist, working on Sundays didn't bother me. She said, "You shouldn't have told me that". I asked her if she meant my saying that I'm an Atheist, and she said yes. Although she always treated me fairly, and we are still good friends 20 years later, it points out how the religious think. It's okay if Christians shout their beliefs to the world, even to the point of knocking on your door, but everyone else is supposed to keep their own thoughts to themselves.

And I'll repeat part of my Prologue statement here. How would a Christian feel if an atheist knocked on his/her door to hand out literature on Atheism? Why is it okay for Christians to knock on people's doors, but not Atheists? I treated the two ladies who knocked on our door in a courteous manner, but how many Christians would treat me the same way if I knocked on their door to distribute literature on Atheism?

Most of us receive religious notes from friends on our computers on a daily basis. When I started putting out Atheistic comments, several people asked me to take their names off my mailing list. They didn't mind telling me what they thought, but they didn't want to hear what I thought. I took them off my mailing list, and also my list of friends.

When this nation was founded, the only religions found in America were Christianity, Deism, Unitarianism, and a sprinkling of Jews and Atheists. Most of the Deists and Unitarians started out as Christians, or at least were raised in that religion, so no one was offended when Christian religious symbols were displayed in the town square. But over the years our country has picked up all of the other religions of the world, plus a large, and increasing number of Atheists and other non-beliefs.

The Graduate Center of the City University of New York published a report in October, 2001 titled <u>Graduate Center Survey of Religion in America Complements U.S. Census</u>. In that report it is stated that the non-religious comprise 14.1% of the population. In 2003, the population of the U.S. was 290,809,777, which means there are at least 41 million Atheists, Agnostics, and other non-believers living in the U.S. And, it is widely thought that 14% is a conservative number. Many Atheists, and Agnostics are hesitant to admit their beliefs because, as I stated earlier, Christians are bullies. Parents are afraid of what their children will face in school if their own beliefs are discovered, and there is not one reader among you that doesn't understand what I am saying here.

Atheists, and other non-believers, together with non-Christian religions make up about 23.5% of the total U.S. population. That means the Christian population in America has slipped from 100% to 75% and is continuing in a steady decline (percentage-wise). The 2008 ARIS Survey shows a steady decrease in the percentage of Christians in America, and a steady increase in the percentage of Atheists. With this shift in religious preferences, it should be expected that one group or another is going to feel as if they are being infringed upon, or pushed around.

Both sides of the religious debate seem to feel that the other side is getting too pushy. The non-religious, and moderately religious feel the Evangelists are going overboard with their religious enthusiasm. And, when the Evangelists get too pushy, the Atheists put up legal bars against these actions, and then the Evangelists feel they are being pushed. They're not being pushed, they're being thwarted in their attempts to push their style of religion on everyone else.

I've already shown that our Founding Fathers did not want any mention of religion at the federal level, and it stayed that way until the 1950s. The religious element seemed to have started when President Eisenhower was baptized as a Presbyterian 12 days after becoming president in 1953.

Francis Bellamy (1855-1931), a Baptist minister, wrote the "Pledge of Allegiance" in 1892. And "Under God" wasn't added until 1954, much to the chagrin of the Atheists, other non-Christians, and Christians who want to keep a separation between church and state. How can a person be expected to make a solemn pledge using words he doesn't believe in? We're still trying to get the Pledge restored to its original wording. Then, in 1956, Eisenhower signed a law that changed the national motto from "E Pluribus Unum" (Latin for "One out of many".) to "In God We Trust".

The Atheists aren't getting pushy, the Evangelists are. The Atheists just want to get back to where we were. When our nation was founded, most of the citizens were Christians, but as I pointed out earlier, our nation was not founded on Christianity.

I will concede that the atheists appeared to be pushy concerning prayer in public schools. Prayers in public schools had been going on since the Mayflower arrived, mostly along the eastern seaboard and deep south. And then in 1960, along came some Atheist (Madelyn Murray), who wanted to stop all that. And even worse, the Supreme Court backed her up!!! I'm sure the Evangelists felt pushed after that decision, but I don't know of any other way to solve the problem. Why should my child be forced to pray in school when I'm trying to teach him/her that there is no one there to hear her prayer. We all know how kids can be bullies, and if my child is obviously not praying, then he/she is in for a lot of harassment. Mrs. Murray filed the lawsuit to stop prayers in public schools because her son was being harassed in school when it was discovered he wasn't praying with the others. If you want your child to pray in school, send him/her to a private religious school. When I was a child, I did not pray in public schools, but I spent part of the third grade in a Catholic school, and of course we prayed then.

During Christmas season 2008, a religious group received permission to set up a nativity crèche in the Washington State capitol building. Shortly thereafter, another group received permission to put up a placard stating that Christianity is a myth. Of course, the religious thought that it was unfair for the atheists to be able to put up their placard next to the crèche, and felt pushed. The courts rightfully said that if you allow one group to express their views on government property, you have to allow all groups to express their beliefs. The state cannot select which group is going to be allowed to express their beliefs at the expense of all others.

That's how the courts feel about it. I look at it a little differently. If it is public property, I own as much of it as everyone else, and I don't want my property to be used to promote personal beliefs. You have your church property, your yards, your autos, and in my town there is even a bill board to proclaim or advertise your beliefs. I don't want to see the nativity crèche, OR . . . the atheist's placards. They are both personal ideas that don't belong on public property. Public property must remain neutral, and therefore must not allow anything that reflects personal beliefs.

There are several instances of the Ten Commandments being erected on government land in several cities over the past several years. The justification for these monuments is that the American justice system was founded on the Judaic/Christian religions. As I pointed out earlier, this idea is erroneous. The court has said that the first Commandment, *"I am the Lord your God You shall have no other gods before me."*, automatically makes it a religious symbol and therefore has no place on government property.

It was shown on TV that the Ten Commandments are displayed in the frieze above the entrance to the U.S. Justice building in Washington DC. That frieze shows the history of law and justice through the ages, and since the Ten Commandments are a part of that history, they belong there. If the Ten Commandments were the only symbol there, I would complain.

Evangelists are complaining about businesses taking Christ out of Christmas, and they're asking everyone to boycott the businesses that do that. (another example of Christians being bullies). Their complaint is that many of the businesses are not saying, "Merry Christmas" in their advertising any longer. Who can blame them?

If they say "Merry Christmas", they are only talking to Christians. If they say "Happy Holidays", they are talking to everyone. What if the proprietor is an atheist? Should he be expected to use religious terms? Yes, I do share presents at Christmas time because I like the idea of sharing presents, but I don't believe in the basis for Christmas. I would be just as happy saying Happy Winter Solstice, since that was the original reason for celebrating during this period. And, as I pointed out earlier, the Puritans outlawed the observance of Christmas, so I don't see what the complaint is all about. If they want to get back to the Christian ways of our forefathers, they shouldn't be in the stores at Christmas time anyway.

I, like everyone else, often receive e-mail that has been forwarded by friends that state something to the effect that since Atheists only comprise 14% of the population, they should sit down, shut up, and let the majority rule. That seems a little pushy to me. Actually, that's a lot of push, and it doesn't fit in with the image of what I thought Christianity was supposed to be. To me, it seems more Islamic than Christian. But Evangelists and the fanatical Muslims are two parts of the same club.

Pushy, and dangerous. They're also very un-American, since they want to trod on the minority.

Were you watching the Republican nominees during the debate in which Governor Rick Perry of Texas tried to belittle Mitt Romney's religion (Mormonism) by calling Mormonism a sect rather than a recognized religion. He said it in a sneering manner and meant it as an insult. Doesn't that sound like the Puritans I wrote about in Chapter 3? Rick Perry is a Southern Baptist, and most of the Tea Party is made up of Southern Baptists. Doesn't that episode sound pushy to you?

6

THE SCOURGE OF RELIGION

I thought long and hard about the title of this chapter. When I thought about writing this book, I was writing down the basic outline of what I wanted to say, and just put down that title because that is what I honestly think about religion. Then, when I actually started writing on this chapter, I thought that the title might be a bit strong and antagonistic. But, it's not, it's just honest. When one thinks of all the people who have died, and suffered solely because of religion, it isn't strong enough.

Think of all the people who died in the Crusades, the Inquisition, the conquest of South America by the Spaniards and missionaries who did their thing with the inhabitants. And in more recent times, the religious war in Northern Ireland, the deaths resulting from actions of Al Qaeda, the Taliban, the infighting between the Sunni Muslims and the Shiite Muslims, and here at home, the Salem Witch Trials, killings by the Ku Klux Klan, the recent killings of abortion providers, and homosexuals, Jim Jones and the kool-aid murders and suicides of the "Peoples Temple" in Guyana in 1978, and on and on and on. Everyone can think of other outlandish episodes concerning religious people and groups. How about all the child molestation by religious figures that we hear of on an almost daily basis? Or the children of the Followers of Christ who die needlessly? Or the harassment in front of abortion clinics? Or 9/11?

You've most likely heard of Terry Jones, that preacher in Florida who burned the Koran in March of 2011, which resulted in the deaths of several innocent people in Afghanistan. Or Bailey Smith's statement in 1980 that, "God does not hear the prayers of Jews.". Bailey Smith was the President of the Southern Baptist Convention when he made that statement. Or more recently, when Governor Rick Perry of Texas tried to belittle Governor Romney's Mormon religion during the Republican nomination debates in 2012. It just doesn't stop.

The Taliban in Afghanistan were so strict, that millions fled the country into Iran and Pakistan. Do you think it couldn't happen in America? IT HAS HAPPENED IN AMERICA!!! That period in American history when the Puritans were in power was just as bad as the Taliban is today. Almost every Evangelist would give a year's pay if there would be religious police in America today like they have in several Mid East countries, and the Evangelists were allowed to be head of that department. If you can find an Evangelist who says he wouldn't, you've found a liar. Who is organizing, and sending the pro-lifers to the abortion clinics? An Evangelist. What is he leading them to do? Repress!! What is the basis for his actions? It sure isn't in the Bible.

You must have seen the Afghan woman who was shot in the back of the head in a sports arena with a large crowd watching a few years ago. It was shown on CNN for weeks. That was one woman who was shot for adultery. The Puritans hung people for practicing Christianity in a different way than they, themselves did. Christians today are killing doctors who provide abortions. Do you really think they are of a different mindset than the Taliban?

Today we need "Bubble Ordinances" to protect pregnant women going to an abortion clinic from religious bullies, who are willing to get physically and psychologically abusive. This, even though the Pro-lifers have no legal or religious basis for their beliefs. They are bullies!! They are supposedly "loving", "caring", and "peaceful" Christians, and yet, they are willing to go out and harass women who have already gone through agonizing moments to arrive at their decisions to have an abortion. And, statistics show that most of the women who have abortions are just as religious as the people who are harassing them.

I was stationed at a radio relay station on a mountain top in the Taunus Mountains near Frankfurt, Germany, where several hiking trails terminate. One day there were three young American women handing out fliers to the German hikers, and so I put my hand out to accept one of the tracts. They were missionaries from some church in America!! One of my German friends also got a pamphlet, and became so angry I thought he was going to burst a blood vessel in his face. He asked me if those girls thought Germany was some third world country with no education. He asked, "Where do they think Luther was from? Don't they even know that the Protestant movement began in Germany? Are they so naively stupid that they honestly think America is the only nation that has the Christian religion?" I've known this man since 1966, and I've never seen him that angry before, or since. Why is the Church sending missionaries to a nation where the majority of the citizens who are religious are already Christian? It was definitely taken as an insult by most of the local citizens.

If you belong to a church, you are not allowed to think for yourself. Their leaders are only looking for sheep that will blindly follow anyone who is willing to lead, no matter where he/she is leading them. Several places in the Bible, and even the religious themselves, refer to the followers of a minister as sheep in a flock. That is NOT something to be proud of!!! It means you are just blindly following whoever is in front of you. No thoughts on where you've been or where you're going, or the purpose of your going there. You're just following. You go to the Sunday sermon, and you mindlessly listen to what the preacher is saying, but do you go home afterward and verify that what you just heard is the correct interpretation of the Bible? Was it taken out of context? Do you go home and read the Bible, or do you study it by looking up the history and background of the Bible on the computer, or in the library? Or do you just accept it as "truth"?

The reason they've settled on abortion for their "cause célèbre" is that everything else about their religion has disappeared. We now know that what separates light from darkness is the rotation of the earth. We now know that the earth is not the center of the universe. We now know that the earth is much older than Bishop Ussher has determined, we now know there were dinosaurs, a fact that can't be explained in the Bible. We now know The Flood was regional rather than global. It's obvious that it is society, not religion, that sets the moral code.

We now know religion has been pushed back so far that they've had to develop a new belief to account for irrefutable scientific discoveries, "The Science of Creationism" or "Creationism" or "Intelligent Design" to explain the world with new understanding. These fanatics have gone through so many mental contortions to match religion with science that they really do look a little silly, if not down right embarrassingly stupid.

"The Bible Is Not Open To Interpretation!!!" I can't remember where I was, but this preacher was obviously an Evangelical Fundamentalist, and was holding the Bible in his left hand while he was addressing his congregation, (it might have been on a street corner somewhere). All of a sudden he slammed his right hand down on the Bible, and screamed, "The Bible is not open to interpretation!! It means exactly what it says!!".

There are many different Christian denominations in the world, and they all interpret the Bible differently. And I'm sure they all feel the Bible is not open to interpretation, and it means exactly what <u>they</u> feel it means.

This is nothing new. Years after Jesus died, St. Paul started sending out letters of Jesus' teachings, (as he had learned them from the apostles.), but he added a few items of his own that were never mentioned by Jesus. And through the years other authors wrote papers on their own thoughts about what was right and wrong. Finally, in 325 AD, Constantine got tired of all the conflicting ideas and rounded up several church leaders and told them to decide on a list of writings that they thought they wanted to have as their authoritative document. That was the first time the books of the New Testament were gathered together in the form we now have. And even the selected books are contradictive in many areas.

We have a friend that explained that she and her husband had finally found the right church for them. She said they had been looking for over a year to find a church that explained things the way they thought they were supposed to be. It was good to hear that they weren't acting the part of sheep, but knew how they wanted to interpret the Bible.

What I'm trying to say is that obviously the Bible means different things to different people, and the whole thing is open to interpretation. In fact, almost every paragraph is open to interpretation. If you google "Bible Concordance" on the internet, and enter any verse you can think of, it will give you all the versions of that verse from the many different Bibles in use today. And if you find the right Concordance, it will give a translation of the original Hebrew, or Aramaic.

The problem with religion is that it is repressive. You are expected to follow someone's lead who has absolutely no idea of what he or she is talking about. The followers follow blindly, and never check out what it is they are following. If the leaders do know what they are talking about, then they are knowingly leading their flock down the wrong path, because what they are saying has no basis in the Bible, or anywhere else. They take selected verses and string them together completely out of context, and come up with something entirely different than their original meanings.

Two weeks after the Haitian earthquake in 2010, that great Christian orator, Pat Robertson opened his mouth again. He said the reason the quake happened in Haiti is because two hundred years ago the Haitian slaves made a pact with the devil. I don't need to say anything. The scourge continues.

7

THE BIBLE VS. SCIENCE

If you believe God created the universe, and everything in it, studying the laws that he set it up with is called science. Gravity, motion, light, earth's geology, and all of the other subjects that we call Science is the study of how He set it all up. You can't say, "Well, I believe in God, so all of that science nonsense is just that, nonsense." It's not nonsense, it's the method he used to set it up so it works the way it does. If you don't believe in God, it still works that way.

In 1654, Bishop Sam Ussher of Ireland (1581–1656) placed the date of creation as Sunday, 23 October 4004 BC. That means the universe is only 6,000 years old, but according to radiometry dating, the earth is about 4,500,000,000 years old. When Bishop Ussher did his calculations, he was using the most up to date technology he had available to him. (Mostly, just math). But just as Copernicus' idea of the sun being the center of the universe had to give way to advances in scientific discoveries, so too Bishop Ussher's theory has to accept the advances in age-dating technology.

The Evangelist will say, "Well, we know it took seven days to make the world, but we have no idea how long God's day is, maybe one of his days is equal to thousands of our years." Since He talked to man several times, His words must mean the same to Him as they do to us. Also, Bishop Ussher used the ages of the generations quoted in the Bible to arrive at his age for the earth. If you want to apply your theory that one of God's days is equal to thousands of our years, you have a long time before you can observe the Sabbath again, because He rested on <u>His</u> seventh day. Do you see what I mean? We all know the earth is older than 6,000 years, but the religious are willing to go through all kinds of mental contortions to match what they know is true with the mythological explanations provided in the Bible. It can't be done.

Today the Catholic church, along with several others, accepts evolution, but the Evangelists are stuck in their deep-rooted religious belief of the Creation. We now have Creationism, The Science of Creationism, and Intelligent Design promoted by those who refuse to let go of their fundamentalist Christian religious beliefs, but realize that science is more plausible than the Bible's explanation.

Another reason they're coming up with these new ideas is that if they can somehow get religion tied into science, they can get religion taught in the schools. It's dishonest, but since it's Christian, it must be morally okay. Right? It's another example of twisting words and meanings to get what you want.

Perhaps the most outstanding examples of the Evangelicals' inability to understand evolution and the age of the earth, rests in two theme parks; Dinosaur Adventure Land, a Christian dinosaur theme park in Pensacola, Florida, and the Creation Museum in Bullittsburg, Kentucky. (The Dinosaur Adventure Land was seized and closed down in August, 2009 because of fines owed by the founder.) Both theme parks taught that dinosaurs and man lived side by side, and they both taught that dinosaurs were taken on Noah's Arc. They can't seem to fathom the size of the Ark and the size of dinosaurs, and don't realize that it would have been impossible. Age dating shows there is about a 3 million year gap between the death of the dinosaurs, and the appearance of mankind on earth.

If you believe the story of Noah and his Ark, there is not just the size of the animals and the size of the Ark to take into consideration, but he would have also had to carry enough food for all of the animals. Not just for the forty days of downpour, but for more than 388 days. That's how long it took for the earth to dry from the 7 days before the flood started when they entered the Ark. And then they would still have to be fed by hand until plants started growing again in enough quantity to feed them after the waters receded. And that would have been a long time, because the soil was salty from the ocean water that had covered it. (Although the waters spilled from the earth and sky, they had to mix with the salty ocean water that was already there, and that would have made all the water salty.) That's just the problem with the plant eating animals. What were the meat-eating animals living on? Since there were only two of each animal. A little rational thought is required here.

If there is a God, and if He made man, then we have to acknowledge that He gave us a rational, thinking brain. If you're reading this and understand what I'm saying, you have a rational brain. You are able to learn, and apply what you learn to the world around you. It seems to me that if God gave you a rational brain, he expects you to use it in a rational way. Believing that man and dinosaur existed side by side is not rational by any stretch of the imagination. Thinking that the Ark could have held two of each type of dinosaur, plus two of every other type of animal that we have evidence for, and enough food to feed them for years, is also not rational.

The Evangelist will say that there is evidence of The Flood all around the world, and every culture has a story of The Flood. No, there is not evidence of <u>The</u> Flood. There is evidence of <u>A</u> Flood. Any land that has a river has experienced a flood at one time or another. Since there was no way to keep time for most cultures in ancient times, there was no way to date most floods. Just because the Native American along the Columbia River in Washington experienced a flood in past times, and the flood was big enough to warrant being made into a tale, it doesn't follow that it is the same flood that Noah experienced.

In fact, the Biblical story of the flood is copied from the ancient Sumerians, and their story of Gilgamesh. There were other sources, such as Babylonian, and Assyrian stories that seem to have been drawn on to compose the Biblical flood story. (All of these cultures were from the Tigris-Euphrates valley where flooding is common.)

Quite often when I'm discussing beliefs with someone, I'll ask them how they know there is a God, and they'll spread there arms to indicate the surrounding environment and ask, "How else could there be so much beauty in the world?" It's beautiful to us because it is all we've ever known. Maybe there are more beautiful things in the universe that we haven't seen yet. Since this is all we have seen, it has to be pretty to us. We feel comfortable in nature, because it is the most pleasant thing we have experienced, but it doesn't mean God made it. It just means it's all we've ever experienced, and we feel comfortable in familiar surroundings. Evolution explains it just as well, and in fact, better than Genesis.

The religious say evolution couldn't work because there is such a large variety of life in the world! They say that, because they don't understand it, and they don't realize the time involved. Evolution is going on continuously, and you can find examples of it all around you. Have you ever heard of someone with 12 fingers and toes? My uncle had 4 nipples.

In plant life, oddities are called "sports". They are all variants on what we call "normal." Nature is always poking in new directions, looking for something else that will work better. This "poking" is not a conscious action on nature's part, but the result of natural occurrences acting on the genes of the eggs and sperm as they are developing. One of the most common examples of evolution that everyone is aware of is the need for a new flu vaccination every year. A new vaccination is needed each year because the flu virus mutates easily. Mutate is another word for evolve, hence mutation, or evolution. If you believe in a strict interpretation of the Bible, and believe we don't mutate, we would all have the same color of eyes and hair as Adam, and Eve. Although we usually associate the word "mutate" with a negative connotation, when talking about evolution it just means a change in the DNA. Either good, or bad.

Most variations are not improvements, but when a good one comes along that increases the chances of survival, then it is accepted and passed down through the descendents, (survival of the fittest). With mankind, this was more true before modern medicine, and the ability to feed non-supporting members of the tribe. With today's medicine, and the ability to support more people, the bad changes are being passed down to our descendants along with the good ones.

Which came first? The chicken? Or the egg? How many times have you heard that question? The egg came first. It was laid by the predecessor to the chicken. During formation, the egg was acted on by a chemical, or a neutrino, or some type of radiation just at a critical moment in development, and the chromosome that was forming was changed ever so slightly, and hatched into a chicken rather than the animal that laid it. And here is one of the main problems that causes the lack of understanding of evolution—it didn't just happen with one change in one egg. At one time, one chromosome would be affected, and then maybe a thousand years later another chromosome would be affected. It took thousands, maybe millions of years for the chicken to go through hundreds, if not thousands of changes to completely change from its predecessor one chromosome change at a time.

Now, this was just one line of ancestry that was described. There were billions of other lines of ancestry that were also being changed, and bred with each other along the same time period. With all these changes cross-breeding down through time, we finally ended up with the chicken we know today.

The Indians of South America, who have lived in the Andes Mountains for countless generations, have larger chests than most people. Their lungs are larger so that they can take in more air, because the air is so rarefied at the high altitudes. It is an obvious example of the body changing (evolving) to meet changing conditions.

The Galapagos Islands is a group of 13 separate islands. It is the location where Darwin noticed the different variations of birds, and these variations finally led to his theory of evolution. The tortoises on each island have also developed (evolved) in different directions, and on one of the islands, a species of pocket mouse has developed (evolved) into two different colors. There are large patches of black lava strewn about the island, and those mice that live on the lava have turned darker to blend in with the lava, therefore making it harder for hawks to see them. (survival of the fittest), and the mice that live on the surrounding soil have stayed light beige in color to blend in with the earth. But the dark and the light can inter breed, so it is the same species. As time goes on, the dark mouse population will develop something different from the beige mouse group, and the beige group will develop something different from the dark group, and they will slowly separate into two species.

This same thing happened in England during the early periods of the Industrial Revolution. There was so much soot in the air that fell on everything, one species of moth started changing colors of gray mottled with a darker gray to blend in with the soot and ash-covered objects around them. This made it harder for birds and other moth eaters to see them. (Survival of the fittest).

The religious will ask me, "If there is no God, where did the universe come from?". And I'll ask them where God came from, to which they reply, "He always was, and always will be." To which I reply, the universe always was, and always will be. They are questions that we'll never know the answers to, but just because I don't know the answer, I'm not going to attribute it to some mystical spirit.

Nature is my god. It answers all the questions I raised previously. It allows for all the randomness that we see in life; i.e. the good and the bad seem to get the same treatment. Sometimes it's good, and sometimes not. But there is no pattern. There is nothing to show that God treats his "believers" any better than atheists, Hindis, or any other non-Christian believer.

8

WHERE DO
WE GO FROM HERE?

I'm sure that by now you must feel that I am against religion, and the religious. Actually, I'm not. I don't believe in religion, and I really don't care what you believe in, but I am adamant against letting the religious get involved in politics to advance their religious beliefs, as we see them doing now.

Our nation has done more for religion than any other nation in the world. We've been able to do this because of our determination to keep religion and politics separate. And because of this separation, our politics have accomplished more than any other nation in the world. In other words, this separation that we've enjoyed for over two hundred years has allowed both the political and the religious organizations, to prosper like no other nation to date.

As I pointed out in an earlier chapter, when religion is in charge, it is the faith of the most ruthless leader that will determine what faith everyone will follow. I mentioned how the Puritans operated, and one only has to look to what is happening in the Middle East today, or look at Northern Ireland for the past 90 years, to verify that what I'm saying is true. Do we really want to go down that path again?

Look at the results of the Tea Party's involvement in the Republican party over the last eight years. The Republican party has completely changed, and is now in complete disarray. When the Tea Party first appeared, it was pushing financial reform, and it was being accepted with enthusiasm. But once it got its foot in the door, it took on a religious connotation, and things have been going down hill for the Republican party ever since. There is no way that a president will ever be elected from the Republican party with its present pro-life demands. Think about it, how many times have we heard, "I didn't leave the Republican party. It left me.", in the last several years.? We've heard it from many prominent politicians, along with the common citizen, and it's a damned shame.

If the Church insists on staying on in politics, I recommend that the Church be taxed. Since it is the church that has started this mixing of Church and state, and since it is the Church that is so anxious to get into politics, I recommend that the Church be taxed the same as all other organizations that make a profit and try to sway political thought. The reason the Church has never been taxed is that it has always been recognized that the churches do so much good in the area of charity, that to tax them would be to take money away from the needy. I agree completely with this thought. I honestly do, but in recent years we've seen a blossoming of mega churches. They really are beautiful works of architecture, with fantastic sound and visual systems. BUT, there is no requirement to disclose how they spend the money they bring in, and therefore, no way to know if there is any money going to charity. (As far as I'm aware.) In fact, I doubt if the Crystal Cathedral in California gave a dime to charity in the last year or two of its existence, before it went bankrupt. I searched the web for more than a half hour, and the only charity program I could find listed was a counseling program for their own congregational members.

If they declared bankruptcy, then they must not have had any money to give away to charity. And if they aren't giving to charity, how can they justify taking in that much money, and spending several millions of dollars to build that mega church without paying taxes? They had a congregation of about 10,000 people at its peak, (Wikipedia), not including the viewers of their daily show "Hour of Power", and still couldn't seem to come up with anything for the needy. It is not immediately apparent that they were giving to charity. I will gladly stand publicly to be corrected if I'm wrong in any of this.

My solution is to tax the Church. Tax the money collected by the Church, and hand the tax proceeds to the state that each church is in to be used to help that state pay for Medicaid. If all churches are taxed at the same percentage rate, the government is not promoting one religion over another, and the monies collected would be used for charitable medical services.

Of course there are some churches that don't earn enough to pay taxes, and provide charity too, and so a higher limit could be set where taxation begins. But, if we tax one church lower than another, some might feel that it is promoting one church over another, and so we should tax all of them at the same rate.

It took me a long time to decide to write this, because of the potential to be offensive to those who are religious, but it is necessary to get religion out of politics if we don't want to go through what our country endured under the Puritans again. Or what we are seeing in the Middle-East countries.

Mathew 22:21 "Render therefore unto Caesar the things that are Caesar's, and unto God the things that are God's." Many scholars think that this refers only to taxes because Caesar's portrait is on the coin that was shown to Jesus when he stated this quote. But I've heard and read that other scholars say it means that you must listen to your government because they govern your life, and God governs the hereafter.

Or, to be more specific, keep them separate because they have separate roles in your life, (and death).

But, since the Church wants to get involved with politics, tax them!!

EPILOGUE

I am not arguing religion with anyone. I think everyone should believe in what they feel comfortable with, and what makes sense to them. To do otherwise is idiocy, if not hypocrisy. And I am certainly not asking you to become Atheists. I've only tried to explain why, as an Atheist, I can stand back and see how religion is beginning to erode our democratic way of government. It's not abortion, the acceptance of homosexuality, or any of the other subjects arising on a daily basis, but religion that is eating away at our democracy. One only has to look at the results of the over-zealous Evangelists on the Texas school board to see how the pursuit of religion is "dumbing-down" the next generation in that state. What I am asking of you is to realize that if you are religious, don't automatically think that everyone else feels the same way you do. Don't try and push your baseless restrictions on others. The results of the last two presidential elections should make you realize that the majority of Americans feel religion and politics should remain separate.

I sincerely want to thank you for taking the time to read my point of view.